*Quick*GUIDES
everything you need to know...fast

Overseas Challenges
Raising Money Through Adventure and Personal Challenge

by Caroline Hukins
reviewed by Clive Miller

WIREMILL
PUBLISHING LTD

Across the world the organizations and institutions that fundraise to finance their work are referred to in many different ways. They are charities, non-profits or not-for-profit organizations, non-governmental organizations (NGOs), voluntary organizations, academic institutions, agencies, etc. For ease of reading, we have used the term Nonprofit Organization, Organization or NPO as an umbrella term throughout the *Quick*Guide series. We have also used the spellings and punctuation used by the author.

Published by
Wiremill Publishing Ltd.
Edenbridge, Kent TN8 5PS, UK
info@wiremillpublishing.com
www.wiremillpublishing.com
www.quickguidesonline.com

British Library Cataloguing in Publication Data
A catalogue record for this book is available from the British Library.

ISBN Number 1-905053-03-7

Printed by Rhythm Consolidated Berhad, Malaysia
Cover Design by Jennie de Lima and Edward Way
Design by Colin Woodman Design

Disclaimer of Liability
The author, reviewer and publisher shall have neither liability nor responsibility to any person or entity with respect to any loss or damage caused or alleged to be caused directly or indirectly by the information contained in this book. While the book is as accurate as possible, there may be errors, omissions or inaccuracies.

CONTENTS

OVERSEAS CHALLENGES

RAISING MONEY THROUGH ADVENTURE AND PERSONAL CHALLENGE

INTRODUCTION

Since the mid to late 1990s, more and more nonprofit organisations (NPOs) are raising money by recruiting supporters to complete sponsored physical challenges overseas. This guide gives a step-by-step approach to organising such events and raises the many issues that need to be considered.

The premise of such events is that participants pay a small registration fee and commit to raise a minimum sponsorship amount for the NPO. From the total amount thus raised, the NPO pays the cost of the trip (for example: hiking the Inca Trail in Peru, trekking across the Sahara desert, cycling the length of Cuba …) and keeps the surplus to fund charitable work. Hence the participant benefits from an adventurous trip at very little personal cost and the NPO raises a large amount of money from a small number of individuals. Overseas events are an attractive fundraising proposition for all these reasons, but they do carry significant risks that must be evaluated and managed. This book tells you how.

Reviewer's Comment
Although the personal financial cost to participants may be small, the commitment of time and effort is considerable. Another major benefit to the programme is the awareness created about the work of the NPO in the community and the media – and of course by the participant.

GETTING STARTED

Before anything else, consider why you want to undertake this type of fundraising, and whether it is right for your organisation.

- ☐ Do senior management and trustees approve?

- ☐ Can the risks be sufficiently contained or managed?

- ☐ Do you have time to devote to the planning and execution of the project, and is it the best use of your time?

- ☐ Will it make money?

- ☐ Will your existing supporters take part?

If the answer to any of these questions is 'no,' those issues need to be addressed before progressing further.

CHOOSING YOUR CHALLENGE

Challenges can involve biking, trekking, horse riding, skiing, canoeing or a mix of any of these. There is no reason not to add more. The two considerations are: Can you find enough people who do the activity? And is it perceived as tough enough for them to raise sponsorship by doing it?

Evaluate your organisation's database of supporters, as they are likely to be your starting point for marketing. Do you want something for the average person e.g., a challenging but non-technical trek? Or are you going for something more extreme (e.g., off-road mountain biking), which would attract a more adventurous person, or a person with special interests?

Either run a trip dedicated to your organisation, or offer supporters the chance to join an 'open challenge,' where participants on the same trip raise money for different causes. There are fewer companies specialising in the latter, so research locally to see if this is possible.

CHOOSING A TOUR OPERATOR

Running the trip itself is a complex and risky business, best managed by experienced professionals. To find a suitable company, gather promotional brochures produced by other NPOs (which should carry the tour operator's logo); visit Travel Fairs; look on the Internet, and in newspapers or travel magazines.

Select an established company with references and a good reputation. They must have company insurance and public liability insurance. Ask to see their brochures, copies of insurance policies, any other necessary legal documents (check local laws), and a copy of a typical contract with an NPO. References from others that have used their services, particularly NPOs, are very useful.

Meet with several companies before committing to one. Questions to ask prospective operators include:

- Do they operate worldwide or specialise in one area?

- What activities do they specialise in?

- Will they sell you a pre-planned trip or design a new one for you?

- How much of the administration do they undertake, and what do they expect you to do?

- How is the pricing structured, and when do you pay which costs? What is included?

- Will you have a dedicated account manager/point of contact?

- How much support or guidance do they provide in the run-up to the trip?

- What level of staffing do they provide on a trip? Is there a doctor, if a trip is strenuous and in a remote area?

- Which other clients (particularly NPOs) are they working with?

- What size group are they accustomed to taking?

- How can they help differentiate your tour from that of other NPOs?

PLANNING

SELECTING A DESTINATION

The single most important aspect of your planning is to select a saleable destination. To do this, consider:

- Which destinations sell well for adventure travel holiday companies?

- Where are other NPOs going?

- Can you come up with a trip that has a tangible achievement, e.g., climbing a mountain, crossing a country, reaching a landmark?

- Is it somewhere that it would be hard or expensive to visit independently, so that this package offers real value?

- What is the perceived value of the trip – is it exotic/exciting/interesting?

- Is it perceived as safe? What does the media say about it? Is it near unstable areas?

- Will you be doing environmental damage by taking a group there?

- What does it cost?

- What is the climate like at the time of year you want to do a trip?

Once you have selected a destination or short-listed a few possibilities, sound out individual supporters, or gauge support through a telephone or email poll. This should confirm whether your choice is likely to sell, or help you decide between two or three options.

LEGAL ISSUES AND RISK MANAGEMENT

If doing this type of fundraising for the first time, it is worth taking legal advice. Find out what the legal requirements and pitfalls are in the country in which your organisation exists. Some areas to consider are: contract between the NPO and the tour operator (responsibilities of both parties before, during and after the tour; accidents on the trip; alternative options should a destination become too risky; protection of participants' data; provision for termination; timing of payments; their public liability insurance; whether minimum numbers are required for dedicated trips; and cancellations.)

- **Risk assessment** – the tour operator should provide a document evaluating the risks inherent in the trip and stating what measures can be taken a) to prevent an incident occurring, and b) to contain the consequences should an incident occur.

- **Regulations** – the flight provider and tour operator should be licensed by the appropriate associations in their country and bonded as appropriate.

- **Promotional materials** – these should carry the logos of the NPO, tour operator, and any regulatory bodies that have approved the tour operator.

- **Contract between NPO and participants** – this will usually appear as conditions on the application form that every participant must sign. (Consider: their responsibilities in preparing for the trip; deadlines for raising money and supplying information; what they must bring; what could result in their not being permitted to take part; cancellation policy; minimum age requirements.)

- **Medical** – participants must declare any existing conditions, any medication they are taking, and any medical history. Sometimes it is appropriate to get a letter from their doctor giving consent to take part.

- **Insurance** – all participants must have travel insurance covering the cost of medical treatment and repatriation, as a minimum. This should generally be taken out when funds are forwarded to the NPO/ tour provider. Failure to do so may leave the participants exposed in the period between payment and departure. It may be appropriate to alert them to the need for other types of insurance, e.g., life insurance, bike insurance.

- **Sponsor forms** – if part of people's donations are being used to cover the costs of the trip, that must be made clear to potential sponsors.

- **Personal risk** – it is rare but possible for death or serious injury to occur on a trip.

- **Financial risk** – if someone is allowed to participate on the basis of pledged donations that do not materialise, the NPO could lose out financially. If this is the case with a high number of participants, the cost could be significant.

Reviewer's Comment

The financial risk can be reduced by collecting all funds from participants prior to departure. If you set out the rules at the beginning, participants will understand what is expected of them and not be unhappy with pre-payment of funds or other rules set out by your organisation.

BUDGET

There are two ways of structuring the fundraising element.

Option 1: Ask participants to pay the full cost of their trip and raise anything they can in sponsorship in addition. The NPO then keeps all the money raised in sponsorship (this could also be an agreed amount), and costs are all covered by the individual's payment. Option 1 most commonly involves establishing a relationship with one particular tour operator, who may also make a donation per client from his or her fee.

Option 2: The individual pays a nominal fee, and commits to raising an agreed minimum sponsorship amount, on the understanding that part of the sponsorship will pay for the cost of the trip. Hence the NPO would receive a total of the initial fee plus sponsorship raised, pay the costs of the trip and retain the difference (though marketing costs would have to be deducted from net profit). Option 2 offers a greater incentive to the individual to take part, but incurs greater risk and cost to the NPO.

This guide focuses on option 2, as it is more complex and offers greater fundraising potential.

Reviewer's Comment

If the NPO is requiring a nominal fee from the participant, it should consider whether this is refundable if the participant does not reach his or her target.

Things to consider

Get a price per participant from the tour operator, and calculate what you'll have to charge to make the trip profitable. Is it saleable at that price? How does it compare to what other NPOs are asking for comparable trips? Remember to factor in all your costs – design of materials, advertising, printing, tour cost, and staff time. The tour cost you pay per person is likely to be fixed. However, when all costs are considered, fewer people will mean greater per-person costs.

When calculating likely income, add together any payment and the average sponsorship amount you anticipate.

If this is the NPO's first challenge, budget for participants raising the minimum sponsorship amount required in order to participate in the trip. In practice they may exceed this, but you cannot rely on this until two or three challenges have happened and your fundraisers have consistently overperformed.

Do anticipate dropouts. Not everyone you recruit will be able to raise the money. Around 15 percent may drop out, due to changes in personal circumstances or problems raising the money. This number may be much higher, especially if a high-profile disaster happens in or near the country you have chosen.

Reviewer's Comment
In my experience, as many as 30 percent may drop out.

You should calculate your breakeven point, i.e., how many participants need to take part and raise the minimum sponsorship in order for the trip to be finically viable.

Aim to recruit more than this to allow for dropouts. Schedule a date for review, when you can still cancel the trip without incurring any costs for places.

These challenges are a relatively expensive form of fundraising. Find out what is an acceptable return on investment (ROI) for your organisation, if there is one. This means how much you will make for funds expended (including staff costs).

You certainly should not spend more on costs than you make as net profit. Ideally, you should be aiming for a return on investment of 1-to-3. Often overseas events are run at a ratio of nearer 1-to-2.

TIMELINE

Allow plenty of time for planning and recruiting participants, and for the people you recruit to raise their minimum sponsorship.

Start planning at least 15 months before your planned departure. It is possible either to buy a ready-made trip that has been done before, or to ask an operator to research a new one. Allow longer if devising a new trip from scratch.

15 months – PLANNING

Consider destinations and discuss them with the tour operator – agree on a provisional price. Have all information and pictures ready, at least 13 months before departure. These will be used to make up the promotional brochure and other materials.

12 months – PROMOTION

Launch the event around 9-12 months in advance of departure (allowing for external factors that may affect recruitment such as holiday season). The brochure, posters, letters, and application form should all be ready for launch date. Have all fundraising materials ready to send when people sign up (i.e., all the contents of the fundraising pack). Review numbers after a couple of months. Is further action needed to fill all the places?

6 months – FUNDRAISING AND PREPARATION

Support participants' fundraising, and send all relevant information to enable them to prepare properly for the trip. Consider a training weekend or information day. Pay a deposit to the tour operator approximately 5 months before departure (timing will vary depending on the company – check their deadlines from the start). Update the tour operator on numbers.

2 months – DEADLINES AND ADMINISTRATION

Participants should pay their first instalment of sponsorship (usually 80 percent of the total) at least 2 months before departure. Medical and insurance information about all participants should be provided to the tour operator at least 6 weeks before departure, along with final numbers and balance of the tour cost.

2 months after trip – FOLLOW-UP
Deadline for all sponsorship should be approximately 2 months after return. It is likely you will have to chase any outstanding monies owed. Evaluate the event fully.

Reviewer's Comment
We would require 100 percent of funds at least 2 months before departure. I find it a waste of time and effort to be chasing funds once the person has taken the trip.

PREPARING MATERIALS

It is vital that the materials correctly convey the nature of the trip, in imagery, text, and tone. Focus on the selling points, and ensure that you have some good pictures. Overseas challenges need a visual image to inspire potential participants and, ideally, testimony from someone who has done it before. Never mislead people into signing up by presenting an unrealistic impression of the trip.

A professional-looking brochure or leaflet is a worthwhile investment. When putting the literature together:

- Include information about the nature of the activity; a day-by-day itinerary; level of difficulty; nature of terrain; climate; costs (including any discounts or incentives); what is included; information about the NPO; and how to apply or find further information.

- Get it approved within your organisation if this is required.

- Get it approved by the tour operator to ensure it is accurate.

- The materials and particularly the conditions of entry should be checked over by someone with legal expertise.

The brochure should be complete in itself and not be misleading. Supplementary information can be provided in an accompanying document, or later via newsletters or email.

At this stage you should also have prepared an application form and any other supporting materials that might convince potential participants to sign up.

RECRUITING PARTICIPANTS

The challenge can be promoted using any or all of the following methods, depending on your budget, and your judgment based on previous experience or advice. Determine when the promotional activity will happen. If you are uncertain whether the trip will sell, start with a cheap means of recruitment, and review results before spending more.

Remember to capture information about how your enquirers heard of the event so you will be able to evaluate each method of promotion for future reference.

Mailings

Mailing your own database of supporters is a good starting point, as warm contacts (people with whom you already have a relationship) attract a far higher response rate than cold contacts (people with whom you have no relationship).

Second, you may choose to buy lists of cold data (information unrelated to your organisation). Define your ideal audience within controlled parameters related to the challenge, or to your organisation or whatever criteria best fit your needs (e.g., ages 20-50, interest in your cause, interest in travel, interest in biking, earning over a certain amount, data less than 12 months old). A list broker can then provide a list of names and addresses fulfilling these criteria. Experiment with different list brokers; negotiate preferential NPO rates; negotiate a refund if not enough contacts who fit within the criteria can be identified.

Remember there will be costs for postage, stuffing the envelopes, and printing or photocopying materials, as well as list rental.

Posters
Posters advertising the trip can be placed by asking warm supporters to put them up (in gyms, workplaces, shops, community centres, etc.), or by mailing them to individuals or organisations cold. Ensure the poster

makes it very clear where further information can be accessed, i.e., by telephone, email or Website.

Email promotion
This is a fast-developing area. Possibilities include: buying lists of email addresses for a cold email promotion; designing an e-flyer and emailing it to your database; or emailing a link to your Website, perhaps as part of your auto signature. Email will no doubt be used in many more inventive ways; it offers huge advantages in cost and immediacy. Online promotion should be coordinated with the rest of the promotion. Ensure you know any laws regarding email communications, including spam (unwanted emails), and follow them.

Advertising
If possible review the performance of advertisements for other similar events. Ask contacts in other NPOs for advice on which publications work well. National press advertising is expensive but more effective if you invest in a series of ads, rather than a one-off. Specify which part of the paper you want the ad to appear in.

Advertising in specialist press is cheaper and better targeted, but publications can be very cluttered with advertisements, and readership is lower.

Include a response mechanism, such as a coupon, telephone number or email address for enquiries. If using a coupon, agree on positioning with the publication so that the coupon appears on the outside edge of a page.

Press and PR

If you have celebrity endorsement, or a newsworthy angle, it should be possible to make a splash. Simply announcing your new event is unlikely to make the papers, unless it is the first of its kind. Ensure all press releases carry the telephone number or email address for enquiries.

If your organisation has media support (e.g., a radio station or newspaper), it is worth asking for free or reduced price advertisements or for the opportunity to run editorial alongside an advert, or to get free PR coverage.

Make use of your organisation's own newsletters and Website, but don't rely on these as recruitment methods.

CONVERTING INTEREST TO ACTION

Only a small percentage of people expressing interest will actually sign up for the trip and go on to raise money. Many people are likely to call or write or email with questions and concerns.

The advertisement should capture their imagination, but now you have to convert them into actually paying a deposit and sending in the signed application form.

Maximise the percentage of conversions by:

- Responding to them quickly and appropriately. Once someone expresses interest, they should quickly receive full information about the trip, application form, and instructions on how to reserve their place.

PROMOTION AND RECRUITMENT

- Having well-informed and enthusiastic people taking calls or responding to emails. Before the trip is launched, ask the tour operator to talk through pictures and answer questions with staff, so that they have a thorough knowledge of the trip.

- Making a note if someone sounds particularly interested, and following up with another call a week or so later.

- Making it easy to sign up. If the deposit is a problem, negotiate paying by instalments. If possible, offer to take payment by cheque, credit card, standing order, or whatever means the potential participant prefers.

Even if people who have expressed an interest don't sign up, you still have had an opportunity to tell them about your NPO. Ensure that the information they receive about it offers other ways they can become involved even if they choose not to go on the trip.

SUPPORTING FUNDRAISING BY PARTICIPANTS

Once the deposit is paid and the application form received, participants will need advice and support to raise the amount of money they have committed to raising.

To help them, send a fundraising pack when they sign up, including advice on any or all of the following:

- Maximising sponsorship

- Running a fundraising event

- Making use of any tax incentives offered in your country

- Approaching companies

- Using the media

- Internet fundraising

- Any legal issues they need to be aware of

Also include sponsor forms, information about the NPO, possibly posters or brochures, and a number to call for help and advice.

As time goes on, keep in touch. Newsletters, phone calls, advice on fundraising, moral support, thanks and appreciation are all important. This helps to minimise a number of them dropping out, and to increase the average amount raised by each person.

Always be clear about the conditions of participation, especially any deadlines by which they need to send money. Let them know what will happen if they do not meet these conditions. Give plenty of notice; remind them; and use a mix of letters, phone calls and emails – everyone has a preferred medium and what suits one won't suit all.

Not everyone will read what you send him or her, so you should speak to everyone who has signed up, well in advance of the first sponsorship deadline. This is to make sure they are aware of the requirements, and to offer practical help if they need it before it's too late.

Support and Preparation

If someone is unable to raise the target sponsorship in the agreed time, they need to be made aware of their options. The NPO will need to decide what these are. Possibilities are: negotiating a different deadline; making up the shortfall of sponsorship through a personal donation; or dropping out of the trip and possibly transferring to another event. The deposit or registration fee is usually nonrefundable in these circumstances.

Tips to maximise income
- Offer incentives to participants to raise more than the minimum amount

- Ensure everyone raises at least the minimum (e.g., ask under-performers to commit to paying the shortfall themselves over a period of time)

- Sell more places and run two trips instead of one to the same destination

- Sell the same trip to a corporate supporter, as a dedicated challenge for their staff

- Get a celebrity to go on a trip, as a draw to recruit more participants

- Offer a discount to individuals who recruit a number of friends to take part

Information about the challenge

It is important that all participants are physically and mentally prepared for the challenge before they go. They will enjoy the trip more if they are able to fully participate, and in remote areas it may actually be dangerous if they are not. Ensure they are given the information they will need in plenty of time, regarding the physical difficulty, the equipment they will need, the nature of camping/hotels, the distances to be covered, the support that will be provided, etc. Including a training schedule in the fundraising pack is a good idea. Also, regular newsletters can remind the group about the preparation they need to do.

An information day or training weekend, two to three months before the trip, will give people time to get excited, raise money, buy everything they need, and train seriously. Prepare a presentation to illustrate what to expect. This also presents a good opportunity to motivate these fundraisers about the cause and the NPO. Send a newsletter or report to those who could not attend.

COMMUNICATION WITH THE TOUR OPERATOR

Update the tour operator monthly on the numbers you have signed up. Your numbers will affect their staffing levels, flight reservations, hotel bookings etc.

Make sure you are aware of the operator's deadlines and what information they will need from you. This may include the following dates:

■ For confirming final numbers

■ For paying the deposit and the balance of costs

■ For providing full names and passport details, medical information, insurance information, requests to change flight dates

■ For providing room share requests, dietary requirements

Although some of this information may be provided directly from participant to tour operator, you need to agree all this from the beginning in order to ensure nothing is missed.

If disaster should strike in the country you have chosen (this could be an act of God, an act of terrorism or the outbreak of a health epidemic), you will need to work closely with the tour operator to effect a solution. It may be necessary to cancel the trip, or it may be possible either to change the dates or change the destination. Look at the risks involved, both regarding participants' safety and potential loss of income and/or reputation to the NPO.

Reviewer's Comment

Review the areas covered by participants' travel insurance and make sure you understand their rights and remedies in these circumstances.

THE NPO REPRESENTATIVE ON THE TRIP

Many tour operators give a free place for an NPO representative providing you recruit a minimum number of participants. The person who takes this place should be physically and mentally prepared for the challenge. This may mean the person chosen devoting time to training. He or she will want to discuss with the NPO whether the training is on his or her own time or as part of the workday. A policy should also be agreed on for his or her expenses, as costs can be incurred buying equipment or clothing for the challenge and/or training.

The organisation will also need to provide appropriate insurance for its representative and obtain anything else required of participants on the trip.

Think about the NPO representative's role on the trip. How will he or she support the participants, and how will he or she maximise this opportunity to spend a week or two with some of the organisation's most valuable supporters?

The representative should be someone well versed in the NPO so that he or she can impart as much information about it as possible when questioned.

Should the NPO representative be from the fundraising department or be someone working in the service-

delivery section? The representative should be able to relate to the other participants, and age or other factors may be a consideration. The ability to relate to a number of strangers who may be under stress on the trek is a useful trait as is the ability to remain cool and relaxed in the event anything goes wrong.

Best advice for the NPO representative: Do not plan to return to work the day after you get back – you will be exhausted!

And be prepared to explain that you've been working, not having a great holiday at the expense of the NPO.

The tour operator will employ a leader to run the trip, and the responsibility is his or hers if anything goes wrong. This means everyone else must respect his or her decisions. They should be trained in safety measures, risk management, and first aid. The NPO representative should participate in the trip as fully as possible, and be seen to add value and work hard. There is a danger of people perceiving him or her to be having a free holiday on their sponsorship money, so it is important to contribute fully.

The NPO representative's role on the trip can include any or all of the following:

- Meet the group at the airport and facilitate introductions

- Act as go-between between participants and the leader

- Manage participants' expectations about what is possible and what conditions will be like

- Support anyone who is finding it particularly difficult

- Try to ensure that everyone is included socially

- Build relationships with participants; make them feel like valued supporters of the NPO

- Find out diplomatically about the interests and contacts that they have, and whether they would be interested in supporting the NPO in other ways

- If someone gets injured, possibly accompany them to hospital, or reassure the rest of the group. Each participant should provide an emergency contact number for someone in their family in case anything serious happens

- Take lots of pictures, especially with NPO branding. For example: famous places, campsites, cyclists/trekkers, meal stops, support crew, animals or porters carrying luggage, terrain, views, and flora/fauna. These can be useful to promote future trips

- Record a video if possible. This is a nice souvenir for participants, as well as a future promotional tool

- On the last night, host a gala night or celebration meal to thank everyone. This may include giving out T-shirts, a speech, an awards ceremony, a cabaret …

- Pass around a book at the end of the trip, so that people can write a few words about what the experience meant to them. With their permission, you could use these quotes to promote future trips

FOLLOW-UP

To make the most of the trip, stay in touch with participants afterwards. Write immediately, thanking them and congratulating them on their achievement. Gently remind them of the next deadline for funds, emphasising how much has already been achieved.

Have a 'debrief' meeting with the tour operator. It is important to let him or her know if there is anything you were dissatisfied with, especially if you plan to run future challenges.

Get the video produced, if applicable, and distribute or sell it to participants. Consider organising a reunion or encouraging group members to do so. There is no financial return on this, but it can help to cement loyalty to the cause.

Any outstanding sponsorship monies will need to be chased, either by phone or letter, or both. People may be required to make up any shortfall themselves, but it is only acceptable to ask this if it has been a clear condition from the beginning.

Evaluate all aspects of the event fully to assist with future planning. Which were effective methods of promotion? When did people sign up? How did they raise money? What did they think of the trip itself? Were there any issues with the tour operator or any other agencies used?

Several months after the trip, send an update informing them of what their trip raised and what the NPO has been able to do as a result. Consider sending participants an annual report to show the organisation's progress. Invite them to other events if it seems appropriate.

These people could be some of the most valuable ambassadors your organisation can recruit, so take steps to keep them involved. It may be a year or several years before they support you again, but the overseas challenge will be an experience they never forget, and some will become loyal long-term supporters.

Do not be afraid to ask them to get involved in other ways.

AUTHOR

CAROLINE HUKINS

Caroline Hukins has worked in the non-profit sector in the UK for over 10 years, both as a volunteer fundraiser and a professional.

Following university, she won a place on the National Society for the Prevention of Cruelty to Children (NSPCC) graduate trainee program in Fundraising Appeals, and subsequently worked on the multimillion-pound Full Stop Campaign for the Millennium. She spent 18 months organizing overseas biking and trekking challenges for Macmillan Cancer Relief, generating over $1 million from this type of fundraising. She then spent three years managing a wide-ranging events program at the National Asthma Campaign, which includied sporting events, overseas challenges, sponsored activities, ticketed special events and wider community fundraising.

Caroline now works as a freelance author and editor, and leads charity treks and bike rides all over the world.

Clive Miller, Reviewer

Clive Miller MBA is an Australian fundraising professional with more than 15 years' experience. He has worked in the areas of HIV/AIDS, overseas aid, and Indigenous health and culture.

In his current position, he has managed the development of an Australian-based overseas challenge program which has raised more than A$650,000 from 540 participants over 5 years. The program, called See The World, is the leader in its field in Australia.